NICK BUTTERWORTH AND MICK INKPEN
THE CAT'S TALE

D1337371

Sometimes, grown-ups find it hard to believe in miracles. In Nick Butterworth and Mick Inkpen's delightful *Animal Tales*, special occasions in Jesus' life are seen through the eyes of some of God's smaller creatures, who have no trouble at all understanding exactly what is happening...

Marshall Pickering is an Imprint of
HarperCollins*Religious*
Part of HarperCollins*Publishers*
77-85 Fulham Palace Road, London W6 8JB

First published in Great Britain
in 1988 by Marshall Pickering

This edition published in 1994

Text and illustrations Copyright © 1988
Nick Butterworth and Mick Inkpen

The authors and illustrators each assert the moral right to be
identified as the authors and illustrators of this work

A catalogue record for this book is
available from the British Library

ISBN 0 551 02878-5

Printed and bound in Hong Kong

Co-edition arranged by Angus Hudson Ltd, London

NICK BUTTERWORTH AND MICK INKPEN
THE CAT'S TALE

JESUS AT THE WEDDING

Hello, I'm the cat who lives next door at number three. I expect you've seen me sunning myself up here on the roof. I like it up here. I can keep an eye on things.

I was up here the other day when a truly amazing thing happened. I knew something was up the moment I saw the servants sweeping the courtyard ...

There I am watching them get ready
for the party. Someone's getting married
and everyone's been invited. It's going
to be the party of the year.

Down below the servants are
hurrying about with tables and chairs.

'Put them here,' says the Steward. He
is the man in charge.

Now out comes the food.

What a feast! There are pies and cakes and roasted meat, all kinds of fish and loaves of bread, there are pots of honey, flasks of wine and bowls piled high with nuts and grapes.

I curl my tail and lick my lips. A piece of fish would be nice

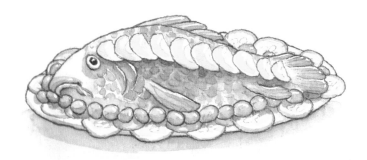

Soon the guests arrive. One or two at first, then lots more, streaming through the gate, laughing and chattering.

One of them is called Jesus. He's come with a big crowd. When he speaks everyone gathers round and listens.

I knew something was going to happen the moment I set eyes on him.

Now everyone is here. The party can begin. I'll go down and hide under one of the tables. Maybe I'll sit on someone's lap and purr for scraps of food.

Everyone is happy. Everyone is laughing and joking. Everyone has a story to tell. Everyone is enjoying the party. Everyone except one woman.

I can hear her talking to her friend.

'Mary! Whatever shall we do? The wine is running out and we've only just begun. What can we give them all to drink? The party will be ruined.'

'I'll have a word with Jesus,' says the other woman. She hurries to his table and whispers in his ear. I follow on behind, ears pricked.

Standing in the courtyard are six huge stone jars.

'Quickly!' says Jesus to the servants, 'fill these jars with water.'

Water? What good is water at a wedding? Wine is what we need, not water.

The servants do as they are told.
Off to the well and back again, with
buckets, jugs and leather bottles.

Splish! Splash! Backwards and
forwards until the jars are full.

One hundred and fifty gallons!
Thirsty work.

'Now draw some off,' says Jesus,
'and drink.'

The woman dips a pitcher in, and
then she gasps! There in her hand is
not the water that the servants brought,
but dark red wine!

Wine! Enough for everyone to drink
and come again.

The Steward tastes the wine and says, 'The best was saved till last!' And everybody cheers and passes round the jug.

So much excitement in one day. I'm off to sleep away the afternoon.

I curl up on the roof, and soon I'm dreaming.

When I wake up it's growing dark.
The guests have gone. The moon is up.
Did the water change to wine or was it
all a dream? Looking down I see the
jars and one of them is still half full.
The moon's reflection in the jar is pink!

So Jesus really turned the water into
wine. What an amazing man. We've not
heard the last of him. I'd bet my
whiskers on it.

If you enjoyed this *Animal Tale*,
you can also read

The Fox's Tale – Jesus is born
The Magpie's Tale – Jesus and Zacchaeus
The Mouse's Tale – Jesus and the Storm